101 THINGS® TO DO WITH

101 THINGS® TO DO WITH
BACON

ELIZA CROSS

Gibbs Smith

Second Edition
27 26 25 24 23   5 4 3 2 1

First Gibbs Smith edition published in 2011
Second Gibbs Smith edition published in May 2023

Published by
Gibbs Smith
P.O. Box 667
Layton, Utah 84041

1.800.835.4993 orders
www.gibbs-smith.com

Designed by Ryan Thomann and Renee Bond
Printed and bound in China
Gibbs Smith books are printed on either recycled, 100% post–consumer
waste, FSC–certified papers or on paper produced from sustainable PEFC–
certified forest/controlled wood source. Learn more at www.pefc.org.

The Library of Congress has cataloged the first edition as follows:
Cross, Eliza.
101 things to do with bacon / Eliza Cross. – 1st ed.
p. cm.
ISBN 978-1-4236-2096-9 (first edition)
1. Cooking (Bacon) 2. Cookbooks. I. Title. II. Title: One
hundred and one things to do with bacon.
TX749.5.P67C76 2011
641.3'64–dc22
2011001925

ISBN: 978-1-4236-6371-3

This book is dedicated to innkeeper and author Gail Riley, who cooks extravagantly delicious breakfasts and uses a well-seasoned cast-iron skillet to fry bacon.

CONTENTS

#57–66 Sandwiches

#67–76 Side Dishes

#77–95 Dinners

#96–101 Desserts

Helpful Hints

- In general, regular sliced bacon is about $1/16$ inch thick and a pound contains 16–20 strips. Thick-sliced bacon is about $1/8$ inch thick and a pound contains 12–16 strips. The recipes in this cookbook call for regular sliced bacon unless otherwise indicated.

- Nitrate-free bacon is sometimes saltier than regular bacon due to processing. Adjust salt accordingly if using nitrate-free bacon for the recipes in this book.

- Artisanal bacon is made from fresh pork bellies that are slowly cured and smoked over a wood fire. Due to its handmade nature, the strips may be more irregular in shape.

- Dry-cured bacon has a more intense pork flavor than regular bacon; it also contains less water and tends to shrink less during cooking.

- Flavored bacons contain additives like apple cider, maple syrup, brown sugar, and pepper. Sweet flavorings may decrease bacon's cooking time and increase the risk of burning, so cook at a lower temperature and watch carefully.

- Bacon smoked over hardwood develops a distinct flavor. Woods such as apple, maple, and cherry give the bacon a slightly sweet flavor, while hickory and oak impart a strong, hearty taste.

- To store bacon, first wrap it airtight in waxed paper or plastic wrap and then cover it tightly with foil. Keep it in the coolest part of the refrigerator.

- For the best flavor, plan to use bacon within 7 days of opening the package.

- Bacon can be frozen for up to 1 month. Thaw in the refrigerator overnight before using.

- To fry bacon, arrange the strips in a heavy unheated frying pan and fry over moderate heat. Use a bacon press to cook it evenly and keep it from curling.

- For easy, mess-proof cooking, bake bacon in a 350-degree oven. Arrange the strips on a broiler pan and cook 15–20 minutes to desired crispness.

- To microwave, arrange bacon strips on four layers of paper towels, cover with two more paper towels, and cook at 70 percent power for about 1 minute per slice, watching carefully to avoid overcooking.

- Bacon cooked at a lower temperature tends to curl less than when cooked at high temperatures.

- For recipes that call for securing bacon with toothpicks during baking or grilling, soak the toothpicks in water for an hour to avoid charring.

- To store leftover bacon grease for later use, cool it to room temperature and pour it through a strainer into a heatproof container. Cover and store in the refrigerator.

- Never pour bacon grease down the drain as it can solidify and cause clogs. Instead, pour it into an old can or other container before disposing.

BREAKFASTS

Apple-and-Bacon German Pancake

MAKES 4 SERVINGS

4 tablespoons	butter or margarine, melted
1	large Granny Smith apple, peeled, cored, thinly sliced
4	eggs
1 cup	milk
2/3 cup	flour
2 tablespoons	sugar
1 teaspoon	vanilla
1/4 teaspoon	cinnamon
1/8 teaspoon	salt
4 strips	bacon, cooked and crumbled
3 tablespoons	packed brown sugar
	maple syrup

Preheat oven to 425 degrees.

Spray a 9-inch glass pie pan with nonstick cooking spray. Add the melted butter to the pan and arrange apple slices on top; bake until apples begin to soften, about 5 minutes.

In a bowl, beat together eggs, milk, flour, sugar, vanilla, cinnamon, and salt until well blended. Remove pie pan from oven and pour the batter evenly over the cooked apples. Sprinkle bacon and brown sugar over top. Bake until center is set and edges are puffed and slightly browned, about 25 minutes. Serve immediately with warm maple syrup.

Bacon, Egg, and Cheese Quesadillas

MAKES 4 SERVINGS

5	**eggs**
	salt and pepper, to taste
1 cup	**grated Colby cheese**
4	**large flour tortillas**
6 strips	**bacon, cooked and crumbled**
1 tablespoon	**butter or margarine**
1 tablespoon	**vegetable oil**

In a nonstick frying pan over medium heat, scramble the eggs and season with salt and pepper; remove from heat. Sprinkle half the cheese over 2 of the tortillas. Spoon the eggs evenly over the cheese-topped tortillas. Sprinkle with bacon and remaining cheese, and top with the remaining tortillas.

Clean the frying pan and heat butter and oil over medium-high heat. Cook each quesadilla for about 1 minute on each side, or until crispy and brown. Drain on paper towels. Cut quesadillas into fourths and serve 2 pieces per person.

Bacon–Hash Brown Quiche

MAKES 6 SERVINGS

3 cups	frozen shredded hash brown potatoes, thawed
½ cup	butter or margarine, melted
8 strips	bacon, cooked and crumbled
2 cups	grated Swiss cheese
½ cup	light cream
2	eggs
¼ teaspoon	salt
¼ teaspoon	pepper

Preheat oven to 425 degrees.

Press hash browns between paper towels to remove moisture and then press onto bottom and sides of a 9-inch pie plate to form a crust. Drizzle melted butter over the crust and bake for 25 minutes. Remove from the oven to a wire rack and reduce heat to 350 degrees.

In a bowl, toss together the bacon and cheese and then spoon into the crust. Beat the cream with the eggs, salt, and pepper and pour over the bacon and cheese. Bake uncovered for 25–30 minutes or until a knife inserted near the center comes out clean. Let stand for 10 minutes before serving.

Spinach and Bacon Quiche

MAKES 6–8 SERVINGS

1 (9-inch)	unbaked pie crust
6	eggs
1½ cups	heavy cream
½ teaspoon	salt
¼ teaspoon	pepper
10 strips	bacon, cooked and crumbled
2 cups	chopped fresh baby spinach
1½ cups	grated Monterey Jack cheese

Preheat oven to 375 degrees.

Line a pie pan with the crust. In a bowl, beat together the eggs, cream, salt, and pepper. Sprinkle crumbled bacon over the bottom of the pie crust. Top with the spinach and cheese. Pour the egg mixture evenly over the pie and bake for 35–45 minutes, or until the egg is completely set. Cut into wedges and serve.

Bacon and Sausage Breakfast Pizza

MAKES 4 SERVINGS

8 ounces	prepared pizza dough
6 strips	bacon, cooked and crumbled
4	breakfast sausage links, cooked and cut into $1/2$-inch slices
1 cup	frozen shredded hash browns, thawed
1 cup	grated cheddar cheese
4	eggs, slightly beaten
3 tablespoons	milk
1 teaspoon	salt
$1/2$ teaspoon	pepper

Preheat oven to 375 degrees.

Press or roll pizza dough into a 12-inch circle and fit in a pizza pan. Sprinkle with bacon and sausage. Top with hash browns and cheese.

In a bowl, combine the eggs, milk, salt, and pepper. Drizzle over pizza. Bake for 20 minutes or until crust is golden brown.

Denver Omelet

MAKES 4 SERVINGS

2 tablespoons	**butter or margarine**
1 cup	**chopped onion**
⅓ cup	**chopped red bell pepper**
⅓ cup	**chopped green bell pepper**
⅓ cup	**chopped orange or yellow bell pepper**
½ cup	**diced cooked ham**
8 strips	**bacon, cooked and crumbled**
8	**eggs, lightly beaten**
	salt and pepper, to taste

Melt butter in a large frying pan over medium heat. Sauté onion and bell peppers until tender. Add ham and bacon and cook for 2 minutes. Add the eggs, season with salt and pepper, and cook until lightly brown on one side. Flip omelet and lightly brown other side. Cut into wedges and serve.

Bacon Bagel Breakfast Sandwiches

MAKES 4 SERVINGS

1 tablespoon	butter or margarine
4	eggs
	salt and pepper, to taste
8 strips	bacon, cooked
4 slices	American cheese
4	bagels, split, toasted, and buttered

Over medium heat, melt butter in a large frying pan and fry eggs to desired doneness; sprinkle with salt and pepper.

Turn off heat; break bacon strips in half and arrange 4 halves on top of each egg. Cover each egg with a cheese slice. Place a lid on the pan and allow cheese to melt.

Use a spatula to transfer eggs to bottom half of bagels. Top with bagel tops and serve.

Bacon Huevos Rancheros

MAKES 4 SERVINGS

4	**large flour tortillas**
1 can (15 ounces)	**refried beans**
8 strips	**bacon, cooked and crumbled, divided**
1 cup	**green chile sauce or salsa**
2 tablespoons	**butter or margarine**
8	**eggs**
1/2 pound	**grated Monterey Jack cheese**
1/2 cup	**sour cream**
1	**avocado, peeled and sliced into 8 sections**

Preheat oven to 325 degrees.

Wrap the tortillas in foil and put in the oven to warm. Heat the refried beans in a heavy-bottomed pan over medium heat and stir in all of the crumbled bacon except 1 tablespoon. Heat the green chile or salsa in a small saucepan over medium heat and reserve. Melt the butter in a large frying pan over medium heat and fry or scramble the eggs to desired doneness.

Remove tortillas from the oven. Spread the bean mixture on each tortilla and top with the eggs. Sprinkle with cheese and top with the warm green chile sauce or salsa. Garnish with sour cream, avocado slices, and reserved bacon.

Bacon-Swiss Breakfast Monte Cristos

MAKES 4 SERVINGS

8	thick slices bread
4 teaspoons	honey Dijon mustard, divided
8 slices	Swiss cheese
8 strips	bacon, cooked
8 slices	smoked turkey
3	eggs
2 tablespoons	flour
1 tablespoon	butter or margarine, melted
$\frac{1}{4}$ teaspoon	salt
2 tablespoons	milk
	powdered sugar
	raspberry preserves

Preheat oven to 425 degrees and grease a baking sheet.

Lay bread on a work surface and spread ½ teaspoon mustard on each slice of bread. Top 4 pieces of bread each with 1 slice cheese, 2 strips bacon, 2 slices turkey, and another slice cheese. Top with remaining slices bread, mustard-side down.

Whisk together the eggs, flour, butter, salt, and milk in a shallow dish until smooth. Dip both sides of sandwiches into egg mixture until lightly soaked. Arrange on prepared baking sheet and bake 8–10 minutes until bottom is golden brown. Turn over each sandwich with a spatula and continue baking 8–10 minutes or until other side is golden brown. Serve warm, dusted with powdered sugar, with raspberry preserves on the side.

Bacon, Leek, and Gruyère Tart

MAKES 6 SERVINGS

1 (9-inch)	unbaked pie crust
3	eggs
1	egg yolk
1 cup	heavy cream, divided
2 tablespoons	butter or margarine
4	large leeks, white and pale green parts cut into ¼-inch slices
	salt and pepper, to taste
6 strips	bacon, cooked and crumbled
⅔ cup	grated Gruyère cheese

Preheat oven to 400 degrees.

Line a pie pan with the pie crust. Cover with foil and add dried beans or pie weights to weigh down the bottom. Bake for 10 minutes. Remove the weights and foil and bake for 5 minutes more.

In a bowl, combine the eggs, yolk, and ½ cup cream; reserve. Melt the butter in a frying pan over medium heat. Add the leeks and season with salt and pepper. Cook, stirring often, until the leeks are soft, about 5 minutes. Add the remaining cream and simmer for 5 minutes more; remove from heat. Combine the leek mixture with the egg mixture. Add the bacon and Gruyère, and stir to blend. Pour into the baked pie shell, reduce the oven temperature to 350 degrees, and bake until the center sets, about 40 minutes. Serve warm or at room temperature.

Cheddar Grits with Bacon

MAKES 8 SERVINGS

1½ cups	quick-cooking grits
3 cups	grated sharp cheddar cheese, divided
3	eggs, beaten
⅓ cup	milk
¼ teaspoon	pepper
8 strips	bacon, cooked and crumbled, divided

Preheat oven to 375 degrees.

Cook grits according to package directions; remove from heat. Add 2 cups cheese, eggs, milk, pepper, and half of the crumbled bacon; stir well. Pour into a greased 3-quart baking dish and top with remaining cheese and bacon. Bake for 20 minutes.

Maple and Bacon Waffles
MAKES 4 SERVINGS

2 cups	flour
1 tablespoon	baking powder
½ teaspoon	salt
1¼ cups	milk
3 tablespoons	maple syrup
2 tablespoons	butter or margarine, melted
5 strips	bacon, cooked and finely crumbled
3	eggs, lightly beaten
	butter
	maple syrup

In a bowl, whisk together flour, baking powder, and salt; set aside.

In a separate bowl, whisk together milk, maple syrup, butter, bacon, and eggs. Make a well in the dry ingredients and add the egg mixture; stir just until combined. Coat a waffle iron with nonstick cooking spray and preheat. Pour ⅓ cup batter into waffle iron, spreading batter to edges. Cook 4–5 minutes or until waffle is lightly brown and crispy; repeat with remaining batter. Serve warm waffles with butter and maple syrup.

Bacon-Cheddar Drop Biscuits

MAKES 16 BISCUITS

2 1/4 cups	flour
2 1/2 teaspoons	baking powder
2 teaspoons	sugar
3/4 teaspoon	baking soda
1 teaspoon	salt
6 tablespoons	cold unsalted butter, cut into cubes
1 1/2 cups	grated sharp cheddar cheese
6 strips	bacon, cooked and crumbled
1 cup	buttermilk
3 tablespoons	butter or margarine, melted

Preheat oven to 450 degrees and grease a baking sheet.

In a bowl, whisk together the flour, baking powder, sugar, baking soda, and salt. Mix in cold butter with a pastry blender or two forks until mixture resembles coarse meal. Add cheese and bacon and stir gently. Add buttermilk and stir until just combined. Drop round spoonfuls of dough, about 3 tablespoons each, onto the prepared baking sheet. Brush biscuits with melted butter and bake 15–17 minutes or until golden brown. Remove from oven and serve warm.

Bacon and Eggs Breakfast Casserole

MAKES 8 SERVINGS

18 slices	white bread, crusts cut off, cubed, and divided
1 pound	bacon, cooked and crumbled
3 cups	grated sharp cheddar cheese
8	eggs
3 cups	milk
1½ teaspoons	dry mustard
dash	hot pepper sauce
½ teaspoon	salt
½ teaspoon	pepper
1½ cups	crushed corn flakes cereal
4 tablespoons	butter or margarine, melted

Arrange half of the bread cubes in a greased 9 x 13-inch pan. Sprinkle the bacon evenly over the top, followed by the cheese and remaining bread.

In a bowl, beat together the eggs, milk, dry mustard, hot pepper sauce, salt, and pepper. Pour the mixture evenly over the casserole and refrigerate at least 4 hours or overnight.

Preheat oven to 350 degrees. Combine the corn flakes and butter in a bowl; sprinkle evenly over casserole. Bake for 1 hour or until mixture is set. Cool on a wire rack for 10 minutes before serving.

Praline Bacon

MAKES 8 SERVINGS

1 pound	**sliced bacon**
3 tablespoons	**brown sugar**
¼ cup	**finely chopped pecans**

Preheat oven to 425 degrees and line two large, rimmed baking sheets with foil.

Arrange bacon in a single layer in pans. Bake for 10 minutes and drain grease. Sprinkle the brown sugar and pecans over the bacon. Bake for 5–10 minutes more or until bacon is crisp. Drain on paper towels. Serve as a decadent alternative to regular bacon; praline bacon also goes great with waffles and pancakes.

Sweet Potato Hash

MAKES 6 SERVINGS

1½ pounds	**sweet potatoes, peeled and cut into ½-inch dice**
	salt
½ pound	**bacon, cut into 1-inch pieces**
1 cup	**diced onion**
1 cup	**diced red bell pepper**
2 cloves	**garlic, minced**
	pepper

Place the diced potatoes in a pot, cover with 2 inches of cold water, and generously season with salt. Bring to a boil over high heat, reduce to medium, and simmer for 5 minutes or until potatoes are barely tender; drain and reserve.

Cook the bacon in a large nonstick frying pan over medium heat until crisp. Transfer to paper towels, reserving about 2 tablespoons of bacon fat in frying pan. Add the onion and cook for 5 minutes or until soft. Add the potatoes and cook for 8 minutes, stirring occasionally, until potatoes are lightly browned. Add the bell pepper and garlic and cook for several minutes more, stirring occasionally, until potatoes are golden brown and bell peppers are tender. Add the bacon and toss. Season to taste with salt and pepper and serve.

Asiago and Bacon Mini Frittatas

MAKES 6–8 SERVINGS

2 tablespoons	butter or margarine, melted
¼ pound	grated Asiago cheese
8 strips	bacon, cooked and crumbled
2	green onions, finely chopped
¼ teaspoon	salt
⅛ teaspoon	pepper
8	eggs, lightly beaten

Preheat oven to 375 degrees and brush a mini muffin pan with melted butter.

In a bowl, mix together the cheese, bacon, green onions, salt, and pepper. Fill about 24 mini muffin cups half full with the cheese mixture. Then pour the beaten eggs over the top, filling the cups to just below the edge. Bake until puffed and lightly browned, about 12 minutes.

Bacon, Cheddar, and Parmesan Muffins

MAKES 18 MUFFINS

2 cups	flour
2 tablespoons	sugar
1 tablespoon	baking powder
½ teaspoon	salt
2 tablespoons	butter or margarine, melted
1 tablespoon	vegetable oil
1	large egg, beaten
1½ cups	milk
6 strips	bacon, cooked and crumbled
1 cup	grated sharp cheddar cheese
⅓ cup	grated Parmesan cheese
¼ teaspoon	paprika

Preheat oven to 400 degrees and grease 18 muffin cups or fill them with paper liners.

In a bowl, whisk together the flour, sugar, baking powder, and salt. Make a well in the center of the flour mixture and pour in the butter, oil, egg, and milk. Stir gently just until blended. Fold in the bacon and cheddar cheese. Fill the muffin cups two-thirds full. In a small bowl, combine the Parmesan and paprika and sprinkle the mixture evenly over the tops of the muffins. Bake for about 20 minutes or until tops are browned and muffins are done.

#19-35

APPETIZERS

Mini BLT Cups

MAKES 24 CUPS

8 slices	white bread
6 strips	bacon, cooked and crumbled
1¼ cups	shredded romaine lettuce
1 pound	ripe tomatoes, cored, seeded, and finely chopped
3 tablespoons	mayonnaise
	salt and pepper, to taste

Preheat oven to 450 degrees and lightly grease a mini muffin pan.

Flatten each slice of bread with a rolling pin and cut 3 rounds from each slice using a 2-inch cookie cutter. Press the rounds into the prepared muffin pan to form shallow cups and bake until lightly browned, about 6 minutes. Cool on a wire rack.

Combine the bacon, lettuce, and tomatoes in a bowl. Stir in mayonnaise, salt, and pepper. Fill each bread cup with a generous portion of the BLT mixture and serve immediately.

Bacon-Wrapped Scallops

MAKES 24 APPETIZERS

12 strips	**bacon, partially cooked and cut in half**
24 (about 2 pounds)	**large sea scallops**

Wrap each half slice of bacon around a scallop and secure with a toothpick. Place bacon-wrapped scallops on a rack in a broiling pan. Broil 4–5 inches from heat for 8–10 minutes, checking and turning several times, or until scallops are opaque throughout and bacon is browned evenly on all sides.

#21

Sweet-and-Savory Bacon Smokies

MAKES 12 SERVINGS

1 package (14 ounces)	**beef cocktail wieners**
1 pound	**sliced bacon, cut into thirds**
3/4 cup	**brown sugar**

Preheat oven to 325 degrees and line a large baking sheet with aluminum foil.

Wrap each cocktail wiener with a piece of bacon and secure with a toothpick. Arrange on the prepared baking sheet. Sprinkle brown sugar generously over all. Bake, turning several times, for 40 minutes, or until the sugar bubbles and the bacon is cooked.

Crispy Bacon and Cheddar Potato Skins

MAKES 6 SERVINGS

6	medium russet potatoes
	vegetable oil
	salt and pepper, to taste
12 strips	bacon, cooked and crumbled
1 cup	grated cheddar cheese
½ cup	sour cream
2	green onions, thinly sliced

Preheat oven to 400 degrees.

Bake the potatoes for 1 hour or until tender; cool. Cut cooled potatoes in half horizontally, and use a spoon to carefully scoop out the insides, leaving a ¼-inch shell. (Reserve scooped-out potatoes for another use.) Cut each shell in half lengthwise.

Increase the oven temperature to 450 degrees. Brush potato shells with oil and sprinkle with salt and pepper. Arrange on a baking sheet and cook for 10 minutes; turn over and bake for 8–10 minutes more, or until potato skins are golden brown and crispy. Sprinkle with bacon and cheese and return to oven. Cook for 2–3 minutes, or until cheese is melted. Top with sour cream and green onions just before serving.

#23

Blue Cheese, Bacon, and Pear Toasts

MAKES 18–24 APPETIZERS

1	thin French baguette
2 tablespoons	butter or margarine, softened
2	Bosc pears, thinly sliced
6 strips	bacon, cooked and crumbled
3 ounces	blue cheese, crumbled

Cut the baguette diagonally in $\frac{1}{2}$-inch slices and arrange slices on a baking sheet. Spread with butter and broil just until lightly browned, about 2 minutes. Divide the pear slices evenly among the bread; sprinkle with the bacon, and top with the blue cheese. Broil until the cheese melts, about 2 minutes.

Bacon Pimiento Cheese

MAKES ABOUT 3½ CUPS

1 pound	sharp cheddar cheese, grated
1 jar (4 ounces)	diced pimientos, drained
½ cup	mayonnaise
2 tablespoons	finely minced onion
1 tablespoon	Worcestershire sauce
dash	hot pepper sauce
¼ teaspoon	salt
⅛ teaspoon	pepper
6 strips	bacon, cooked and crumbled

In a bowl, combine cheese, pimientos, mayonnaise, onion, Worcestershire sauce, pepper sauce, salt, and pepper and stir gently. Fold in the crumbled bacon just until blended. Serve as a spread with crackers or vegetables.

Bacon and Swiss Mini Tarts

MAKES 16 TARTS

8 strips	**bacon, cooked and crumbled**
1	**tomato, chopped**
¼ cup	**finely minced onion**
¾ cup	**grated Swiss cheese**
½ cup	**mayonnaise**
1 tablespoon	**chopped fresh basil (or 1 teaspoon dried basil)**
1 can (16 ounces)	**refrigerated flaky buttermilk biscuits**

Preheat oven to 375 degrees and grease a mini muffin pan.

In a bowl, combine bacon, tomato, onion, cheese, mayonnaise, and basil. Separate biscuits horizontally and press halves into mini muffin pan. Fill each biscuit half with some of the bacon mixture. Bake for 10–12 minutes, or until golden brown.

Bacon-Stuffed Mushrooms
MAKES 18 APPETIZERS

18	medium button mushrooms
6 strips	bacon
⅓ cup	finely minced onion
3 tablespoons	mayonnaise
½ cup	grated Parmesan cheese

Preheat oven to 350 degrees and grease a baking sheet.

Clean mushrooms, then remove and finely chop the stems; reserve.

In a frying pan, cook bacon until crisp. Remove bacon, drain on paper towels, and crumble. Discard all but 2 tablespoons drippings from pan. Sauté chopped mushroom stems and onion in bacon drippings over medium heat until tender.

In a bowl, combine bacon, mushroom-and-onion mixture, mayonnaise, and cheese; fill mushroom caps with stuffing mixture. Arrange mushrooms on the prepared baking sheet. Bake for 15–20 minutes, or until hot and cheese is melted.

Bacon-Cheddar Jalapeño Poppers

MAKES 6 SERVINGS

2 cups	**grated cheddar cheese**
4 ounces	**cream cheese, softened**
6	**jalapeño peppers, seeded and halved**
12 strips	**bacon, partially cooked**

Preheat the broiler and line a baking sheet with aluminum foil.

In a bowl, combine cheddar and cream cheese and mix well. Spread cheese mixture evenly in jalapeño halves. Wrap each half with a bacon slice and secure with a toothpick if necessary. Arrange on the prepared baking sheet and broil 4–5 minutes, turning once, until bacon is crispy.

Cheesy Bacon Rolls

MAKES 32 APPETIZERS

2 cans	**refrigerated crescent rolls**
3 ounces	**cream cheese, softened**
1 cup	**grated sharp cheddar cheese**
¼ cup	**grated Parmesan cheese**
8 strips	**bacon, cooked and crumbled**
2 tablespoons	**butter or margarine, melted**

Preheat oven to 375 degrees and line a baking sheet with parchment paper.

Unroll crescent rolls and separate dough into 8 rectangles, pressing along diagonal perforations to seal.

In a bowl, combine cream cheese, cheddar cheese, Parmesan, and bacon. Spread the mixture evenly on the dough rectangles and, starting at the short end, roll up like a jelly roll. Cut each roll into 4 slices and arrange on the prepared baking sheet. Brush with the melted butter. Bake for 11–13 minutes or until lightly browned.

Chèvre-Stuffed Dates

MAKES 12 SERVINGS

½ **pound**	**sliced bacon**
1 **pound**	**pitted dates**
4 **ounces**	**goat cheese (or cream cheese)**
1 **bunch**	**fresh basil, leaves washed and stems removed**

Preheat oven to 350 degrees.

Cut the bacon strips in half; set aside. Split the dates lengthwise and stuff with a heaping teaspoon of goat cheese. Press halves back together and wrap each date with a basil leaf and a bacon strip. Secure with toothpicks and place in a single layer on a baking sheet. Bake for 15–20 minutes, turning once, until the bacon is crispy. Remove from oven, drain on paper towels, and transfer to a serving platter.

Ultimate Snack Mix

MAKES 12 SERVINGS

6 strips	bacon
¼ cup	butter, melted
2 tablespoons	Worcestershire sauce
1¼ teaspoons	seasoned salt
¼ teaspoon	garlic salt
4 cups	crunchy corn squares cereal
2 cups	crunchy wheat squares cereal
2 cups	crunchy rice squares cereal
2 cups	potato stick snacks
1 cup	crushed bugle-shaped corn snacks
1 cup	rye chips
1 cup	honey mustard pretzel chunks
1 cup	Baby Goldfish cheese crackers
½ cup	blanched almonds

Preheat oven to 275 degrees.

Cook the bacon in a large frying pan over medium heat until brown and crispy. Remove and drain on paper towels.

Combine the bacon drippings, butter, Worcestershire sauce, seasoned salt, and garlic salt in a large bowl. Add the remaining ingredients and stir until all pieces are coated. Spoon onto two large, rimmed baking sheets and bake for 40 minutes, stirring every 10 minutes. Let cool completely before storing in the refrigerator, covered, and bring to room temperature before serving.

Parmesan-Bacon Crackers

MAKES 36 CRACKERS

36	buttery rectangular crackers
½ cup	grated Parmesan cheese
12 strips	bacon, cut into thirds

Preheat oven to 250 degrees.

Arrange the crackers in a single layer on two baking sheets. Sprinkle each cracker with a generous teaspoon of cheese and top with 1 slice bacon. Bake for 1 hour, or until bacon is browned and crisp. Drain on paper towels and serve warm.

#32

Bacon Popcorn

MAKES 4 SERVINGS

10 strips	bacon, diced
⅓ cup	popcorn kernels
	salt (optional)

Cook the bacon in a large, heavy saucepan over medium heat until brown and crispy. Remove the bacon with a slotted spoon. Add a few popcorn kernels to the bacon drippings and wait for one to pop. Then add the remaining popcorn, cover the pan with a lid, and shake while the rest of the popcorn pops. Remove from heat and add the diced bacon to the popcorn. Toss and sprinkle with salt, if desired.

Bacon Meatballs

MAKES 18 MEATBALLS

¹⁄₂ cup	barbecue sauce
¹⁄₂ cup	grape jelly
18	precooked Italian-style meatballs
9 strips	bacon, cut in half
1¹⁄₂ tablespoons	brown sugar
¹⁄₄ teaspoon	pepper

Preheat oven to 350 degrees. Line a baking sheet with foil and spray with nonstick cooking spray.

In a small saucepan, combine barbecue sauce and grape jelly. Cook over medium heat for about 5 minutes, stirring until blended; remove from heat and reserve. Wrap each meatball with a half strip of bacon and secure with a toothpick; trim off any excess and reserve for another use. Place meatballs on the prepared baking sheet.

In a small bowl, combine the brown sugar and pepper and sprinkle over the meatballs. Bake for 10 minutes. Turn meatballs over and cook 10 minutes more, or until the bacon is crispy. Remove from oven, drain on paper towels, and transfer to a serving platter.

Bacon Tater Treats
MAKES 10–12 SERVINGS

½ cup	**ketchup**
½ cup	**mayonnaise**
40	**frozen tater tots**
20 strips	**bacon, cut in half**

Preheat oven to 400 degrees.

In a bowl, combine ketchup and mayonnaise; reserve. Thaw tater tots for 15–20 minutes, or defrost in microwave for 1 minute. Wrap each tater tot with a half slice of bacon and secure with a toothpick; trim off any extra and reserve for another use. Stand the bacon-wrapped tater tots upright on a rimmed baking sheet and bake for 10 minutes. Turn sideways and cook for 5 minutes; flip over and cook 5 minutes more, or until brown and crispy. Drain on paper towels and serve.

Hot Bacon Dip

MAKES 8 SERVINGS

1 cup	mayonnaise
1 cup	sour cream
1 package (8 ounces)	cream cheese, softened
1 cup	grated sharp cheddar cheese
⅓ cup	grated Parmesan cheese
2	green onions, finely chopped
1 pound	bacon, cooked and crumbled
1 jar (4 ounces)	diced pimientos, drained
	assorted crackers or corn chips

Preheat oven to 350 degrees and grease a 1-quart casserole dish.

In a bowl, combine mayonnaise, sour cream, cheeses, and green onions. Fold in bacon and pimientos and spoon into the prepared casserole dish. Bake, uncovered, for 20 minutes. Remove from oven and serve with crackers or corn chips.

SOUPS

Corn, Bacon, and Jack Chowder

MAKES 6 SERVINGS

6 strips	bacon, diced
1	large onion, chopped
4 cups	corn
3½ cups	chicken stock or broth
1 teaspoon	salt
¼ teaspoon	pepper
1 cup	grated Monterey Jack cheese
1 cup	heavy cream
dash	hot pepper sauce

In a large, heavy pot, fry bacon until crisp. Remove with a slotted spoon, drain on paper towels, and reserve. Add the onion to the drippings and cook, stirring often, until translucent, about 4 minutes. Add the corn and cook 4 minutes more. Add the stock, salt, and pepper and heat until almost boiling. Reduce heat to low and simmer for 15 minutes.

Ladle half of the soup into a food processor or blender and purée. Return the blended mixture to the pot and keep over low heat. Add the cheese, a little at a time, stirring and allowing each addition to melt completely before adding more. Slowly pour in the cream. Heat for a few more minutes, add the hot pepper sauce, and check the seasonings.

Ladle the soup into bowls and sprinkle bacon over each bowl. Serve immediately.

Split Pea Soup

MAKES 8–10 SERVINGS

1 pound	dry split peas, rinsed and picked over
8 cups	water
1	meaty ham bone
½ pound	lean smoked slab bacon
1 cup	chopped onion
2	large celery stalks, chopped
1	large carrot, diced
1 cup	dry white wine (or vegetable broth)
1 clove	garlic, minced
½ teaspoon	dried marjoram
¼ teaspoon	dried thyme
	salt and pepper, to taste
8 strips	bacon, cooked and crumbled

In a large, heavy saucepan, combine the peas, water, ham bone, slab bacon, onion, celery, carrot, wine, garlic, marjoram, and thyme. Bring the mixture to a boil over medium-high heat. Reduce the heat to low, cover, and simmer, stirring occasionally, adding additional water if needed, until the peas are soft, about 2½ hours. Remove the bacon slab and ham bone to a cutting board and cool. When the meat is cool enough to handle, chop any lean meat and return to the soup; discard the remainder. Continue to simmer the soup about 15–20 minutes more. Season with salt and pepper and garnish soup with crumbled bacon.

Loaded Baked Potato Soup

MAKES 8 SERVINGS

4	large russet potatoes
1 cup	sour cream
½ cup	butter or margarine, melted
3 cups	whole milk
1 teaspoon	salt
½ teaspoon	pepper
4	green onions, thinly sliced
1 cup	grated sharp cheddar cheese
8 strips	bacon, cooked and crumbled

Preheat oven to 400 degrees.

Prick potatoes with a fork and bake until tender, about 1 hour. Cool, peel, and cut potatoes into 1-inch pieces. Transfer to a large stockpot and mash with sour cream and butter until smooth. Add the milk, salt, and pepper and bring the soup to a simmer over medium heat. Divide among bowls and serve garnished with green onions, cheese, and bacon.

Texas-Style Slow Cooker Beef Chili

MAKES 8 SERVINGS

6 strips	**bacon, chopped**
2 pounds	**boneless cubed beef**
2 cans (15 ounces each)	**chili beans, drained**
1 can (28 ounces)	**crushed tomatoes**
1 can (8 ounces)	**tomato sauce**
1	**onion, finely chopped**
1 can (4 ounces)	**diced green chiles**
2 cloves	**garlic, minced**
3 tablespoons	**chili powder**
1½ teaspoons	**ground cumin**
	salt and pepper

Fry bacon until crisp; remove with a slotted spoon and drain on paper towels. Brown half the beef cubes in the pan with bacon drippings, about 5 minutes. Drain and transfer to a 3½- to 4-quart slow cooker. Repeat with remaining meat. Stir bacon and remaining ingredients into slow cooker; cover and cook on low heat for 8 hours, or until beef is tender.

Sweet Potato Soup

MAKES 4–6 SERVINGS

6 strips	**bacon, diced**
1	**onion, finely chopped**
2	**celery stalks, chopped**
1	**large leek, white and pale green parts only, thinly sliced**
2 cloves	**garlic, minced**
1½ pounds	**sweet potatoes, peeled and cut into 1-inch cubes**
5 cups	**chicken stock or broth**
1½ cups	**half-and-half**
2 tablespoons	**maple syrup**
	salt and pepper, to taste

In a large, heavy pot, fry bacon until crisp, remove with a slotted spoon, and drain on paper towels; reserve. Add the onion and sauté until translucent, about 5 minutes. Add the celery and leek and sauté for 5 minutes more. Add the garlic and sauté for 1 minute. Add the potatoes and stock and bring to a boil. Reduce heat and simmer, uncovered, until potatoes are tender, about 20–25 minutes. Purée in a blender or food processor until smooth, working in batches if necessary. Return the soup to the saucepan. Add the half-and-half and maple syrup and heat, stirring frequently. Season with salt and pepper. Ladle the soup into bowls and garnish each with bacon.

New England Clam Chowder

MAKES 8 SERVINGS

3 cans (6.5 ounces each)	minced clams
1 cup	water
1	onion, chopped
1 cup	diced celery
2 cups	peeled and cubed potatoes
½ cup	diced carrots
½ cup	butter or margarine
¾ cup	flour
4 cups	half-and-half
	salt and pepper, to taste
6 strips	bacon, cooked and crumbled

Drain juice from clams into a large pan and add water; cook over medium heat until simmering. Add the onion, celery, potatoes, and carrots and cook until tender, about 10–15 minutes.

Meanwhile, in a large, heavy saucepan, melt the butter over medium heat. Whisk in flour until smooth. Whisk in half-and-half and stir constantly until thick and smooth. Stir in vegetable mixture and cook, stirring constantly, for 3 minutes. Stir in clams and cook for 2 minutes; season with salt and pepper. Serve at once, garnished with bacon crumbles.

Fast and Easy Minestrone

MAKES 8 SERVINGS

6 strips	bacon, chopped
1	onion, finely chopped
1 clove	garlic, minced
4 cups	hot water
2 cups	chicken stock or broth
1 jar (26 ounces)	marinara sauce
1 can (15 ounces)	cannellini beans, drained
1 bag (16 ounces)	Italian blend frozen vegetables, thawed
½ cup	small dry pasta
1 teaspoon	dried oregano
	salt and pepper, to taste

In a large saucepan or Dutch oven, sauté the bacon and onion over medium heat until bacon is browned and onion is translucent; add garlic and cook for 1 minute more. Add remaining ingredients and stir. Cook for 30 minutes, or until pasta is tender.

Creamy Artichoke Soup

MAKES 4 SERVINGS

1 package (9 ounces)	frozen artichoke hearts, cooked according to directions and drained
1	medium leek, white and pale green parts only, thinly sliced
4 cups	chicken stock or broth
½ cup	heavy cream
	salt and pepper, to taste
6 strips	bacon, cooked and crumbled

Put the artichokes, leek, and stock in a large pot and bring to a boil. Reduce the heat, cover, and simmer for about 10 minutes. Remove from heat and cool for 5 minutes. Pour the mixture in a food processor or blender and process until smooth; return to pot. Add the cream, salt, and pepper and stir until well combined. Heat through and ladle into warmed soup bowls, garnishing with bacon.

Butter Bean, Leek, and Bacon Soup

MAKES 8 SERVINGS

6 strips	bacon, chopped
1 cup	chopped onion
2	leeks, white and pale green parts only, sliced
2 cloves	garlic, minced
2 cans (15 ounces each)	butter beans, drained
¼ teaspoon	dried thyme
3 cups	chicken stock or broth
1 cup	half-and-half
¼ cup	chopped fresh parsley
2 teaspoons	lemon juice
	salt and pepper, to taste

In a large saucepan over medium heat, sauté the bacon until browned, remove with a slotted spoon, and drain on paper towels; reserve. Add the onion, leeks, and garlic and sauté for about 5 minutes over medium-high heat. Add the beans, thyme, and stock; simmer 20 minutes.

Purée soup in batches in blender or food processor. When smooth, return to saucepan and add the half-and-half; heat through. Before serving, stir in chopped parsley, lemon juice, salt, and pepper. Garnish with bacon.

Cream of Mushroom Soup

MAKES 6 SERVINGS

8 strips	bacon
1 pound	button mushrooms, sliced
¼ cup	butter or margarine
1	large onion, chopped
1 clove	garlic, minced
¼ cup	flour
4 cups	chicken stock or broth
	salt and pepper, to taste
1 cup	cream

In a large saucepan over medium heat, sauté the bacon until browned. Remove bacon, drain on paper towels, and crumble, reserving 2 tablespoons bacon fat in pan. Add the mushrooms and cook for 5 minutes until lightly browned. Remove from the pan with a slotted spoon; reserve.

Add butter to the pan and heat until melted. Add onion and garlic and cook for 5 minutes or until onions are softened. Sprinkle with flour and cook, stirring constantly, for 2 minutes or until mixture is bubbling. Stir in the stock and cook until mixture is thickened. Add mushrooms and bring to a boil. Season with salt and pepper and simmer for 20 minutes. Add the cream and cook just until heated through. Serve garnished with bacon.

Hearty Beef and Bacon Stew

MAKES 6 SERVINGS

1 (2½- to 3-pound)	boneless beef chuck pot roast, cut into 1½-inch cubes
⅓ cup	flour
6 strips	bacon
½ pound	sliced mushrooms
1	medium onion, chopped
3 cups	beef stock or broth
¼ cup	red wine (or additional beef stock)
½ teaspoon	dried thyme, crushed
¼ teaspoon	pepper
3	medium carrots, cut into 1-inch pieces
1	large russet potato, peeled and cut into ½-inch pieces
1 cup	frozen peas

Preheat oven to 325 degrees. In a bowl or ziplock plastic bag, sprinkle meat with flour and toss to coat; reserve.

In a large Dutch oven, cook bacon over medium heat until crisp. Remove bacon, drain on paper towels, and crumble; reserve 3 tablespoons bacon fat in pan. Brown meat in two batches in the hot drippings over medium heat; transfer to a heated dish and reserve. Add the mushrooms and onion; cook until tender. Return meat to pan; add bacon, stock, wine, thyme, pepper, carrots, and potato and bring to a boil. Remove from heat, cover, and bake for 2½ hours, or until meat is tender. Stir in frozen peas; cover and return to oven for 15 minutes more.

SALADS

Baby Spinach Salad with Hot Bacon Dressing

MAKES 4 SERVINGS

8 strips	**bacon**
3 tablespoons	**red wine vinegar**
1 teaspoon	**sugar**
½ teaspoon	**Dijon mustard**
	salt and pepper, to taste
½ pound	**baby spinach, washed and stems removed**
1	**small red onion, thinly sliced**
2	**hard-boiled eggs, peeled and sliced**
1 cup	**grated mozzarella cheese**

In a large sauté pan over medium heat, fry bacon until crispy. Remove from pan and drain, reserving 3 tablespoons bacon fat. Crumble the bacon and reserve. Reduce the heat to low and whisk in the red wine vinegar, sugar, and Dijon mustard. Season with salt and pepper.

Combine the spinach and sliced onion in a large bowl and toss. Add the dressing and bacon and toss to combine. Divide the spinach among plates or bowls and evenly divide the egg among them. Sprinkle with the cheese and serve.

Cobb Salad

MAKES 4 SERVINGS

½ head	romaine lettuce, chopped
½ head	iceberg lettuce, cored and chopped
3	hard-boiled eggs, peeled and chopped
2	tomatoes, seeds removed and chopped
1	large boneless skinless chicken breast, cooked and cut into ½-inch cubes
1	avocado, peeled and cut into ½-inch cubes
2 ounces	Roquefort cheese, crumbled
8 strips	bacon, cooked and crumbled
	Italian or other favorite salad dressing
	salt and pepper, to taste

Combine the lettuces and place on a serving platter. Making neat rows, top the greens with the eggs, tomatoes, chicken, avocado, cheese, and bacon. To serve, drizzle salad with dressing and season with salt and pepper.

Hot German Potato Salad

MAKES 4 SERVINGS

3 cups	peeled and diced potatoes
6 strips	bacon
1	small onion, diced
¼ cup	white vinegar
2 tablespoons	water
3 tablespoons	sugar
1 teaspoon	salt
⅛ teaspoon	pepper
1 tablespoon	chopped fresh parsley

Place the potatoes in a pot and fill with enough water to cover. Bring to a boil and cook for about 10 minutes, or until easily pierced with a fork; drain and set aside to cool.

Fry the bacon in a large frying pan over medium-high heat until browned and crisp. Remove the bacon, drain, and crumble. Add the onion to the bacon drippings and cook over medium heat until browned. Add the vinegar, water, sugar, salt, and pepper to the pan and whisk until combined. Bring to a boil, then add the potatoes and parsley. Crumble in half of the bacon. Heat through, then transfer to a serving dish. Crumble the remaining bacon over top and serve warm.

Red Potato Salad

MAKES 6 SERVINGS

2 pounds	**small red potatoes**
³/4 cup	**mayonnaise**
¹/3 cup	**sour cream**
8 strips	**bacon, cooked and crumbled**
3 to 4	**hard-boiled eggs, diced**
2	**celery stalks, diced**
2	**green onions, thinly sliced**
2 tablespoons	**diced dill pickle**
	salt and pepper

Slice the potatoes in ½-inch slices and place in a medium saucepan. Cover with water and boil for about 10–12 minutes until just tender; drain and cool.

In a large bowl, whisk together the mayonnaise and sour cream. Add the potatoes, bacon, eggs, celery, green onions, and pickle. Stir gently to combine and season to taste with salt and pepper.

Chicken and Bacon Caesar Salad

MAKES 4 SERVINGS

1 head	**romaine lettuce, cut into bite-sized pieces**
¹⁄₂ cup	**Caesar salad dressing**
6 strips	**bacon, cooked and crumbled**
¹⁄₄ cup	**grated Parmesan cheese**
2 cups	**cooked chopped chicken breast**
1 cup	**croutons**

In a large bowl, toss the lettuce with the salad dressing, bacon, and cheese. Mound the salad on chilled salad plates and then divide the chicken among the plates and top with croutons.

Chopped Salad

MAKES 6 SERVINGS

1 head	romaine lettuce, chopped
½ head	iceberg lettuce, chopped
2 tablespoons	thinly sliced fresh basil
1	medium tomato, cored and cut into ¼-inch dice
2 ounces	Gorgonzola cheese, crumbled
½ cup	sliced black olives, drained
1 cup	canned garbanzo beans, drained
1	avocado, peeled and diced
6 strips	bacon, cooked and crumbled
⅓ to ½ cup	creamy Italian dressing

Combine the lettuces and basil in a large bowl and toss. Add the tomato, Gorgonzola, olives, beans, avocado, and bacon and toss gently. Drizzle ¼ cup of the dressing over top and toss gently. Add additional dressing to taste and serve.

Ranch Pasta Salad

MAKES 6 SERVINGS

12 ounces	**uncooked spiral pasta**
1 cup	**mayonnaise**
3 tablespoons	**dry ranch salad dressing mix**
½ cup	**milk**
12 strips	**bacon, crisply fried, drained, and crumbled**
1	**large tomato, chopped**
1 can (4.25 ounces)	**sliced black olives, drained**
⅓ cup	**finely chopped celery**
1 cup	**grated sharp cheddar cheese**
¼ cup	**finely chopped flat-leaf parsley**

Bring a large pot of lightly salted water to a boil and add the pasta. Meanwhile, combine the mayonnaise, ranch dressing mix, and milk in a large bowl and stir until smooth.

When the pasta is al dente, drain and cool briefly, then add to the bowl with the dressing and mix gently. Add the bacon, tomato, olives, celery, and cheese and gently fold to coat with dressing. Cover and chill for at least 1 hour in the refrigerator. Add the chopped parsley just before serving.

Spring Pea Salad

MAKES 8 SERVINGS

½ cup	mayonnaise
½ cup	sour cream
2	hard-boiled eggs, peeled and finely chopped
1 bag (32 ounces)	frozen petite peas, thawed
1 cup	chopped celery
8 strips	bacon, cooked and crumbled
1 cup	grated cheddar cheese
½ cup	sunflower seeds
	salt and pepper, to taste

In a bowl, combine the mayonnaise and sour cream and stir until well blended. Fold in the eggs, followed by the remaining ingredients, and adjust seasonings if needed.

BLT Salad

MAKES 6 SERVINGS

2 tablespoons	**olive oil**
1 clove	**garlic, minced**
¼ teaspoon	**salt**
4 slices	**whole-grain bread, cut into ½-inch cubes**
3	**romaine lettuce hearts, coarsely chopped**
1 pint	**grape tomatoes, halved**
1	**ripe avocado, peeled and chopped**
½	**small red onion, thinly sliced (optional)**
⅓ to ½ cup	**ranch salad dressing**
10 strips	**bacon, cooked, drained, and crumbled**

Preheat oven to 350 degrees.

Combine the oil, garlic, and salt in a large bowl; add bread cubes and toss to coat. Transfer to a baking sheet and bake until golden brown, about 10–12 minutes. Remove pan from oven and cool on a wire rack. (Croutons can be made 1 day ahead. Store in an airtight container at room temperature.)

In a large bowl, combine the lettuce, tomatoes, avocado, and onion, if using. Add the dressing and toss gently. Divide the salad evenly among salad plates and top with bacon and croutons.

Crunchy Bacon Cauliflower Salad

MAKES 8 SERVINGS

1 cup	mayonnaise
1 teaspoon	white wine vinegar
⅓ cup	sugar
3 tablespoons	milk
1 pound	bacon, cooked and crumbled
1 head	iceberg lettuce, torn into bite-sized pieces
4 cups	chopped fresh cauliflower florets
1 cup	grated Parmesan cheese

In a small bowl, combine the mayonnaise, vinegar, sugar, and milk and stir until well blended; reserve.

In a large bowl, combine the bacon, lettuce, cauliflower, and cheese. Drizzle the salad dressing over top and toss gently. Serve immediately.

SANDWICHES

Kentucky Hot Browns

MAKES 6 SERVINGS

6	French baguette rolls, split in half
12 strips	bacon, cooked
1½ pounds	sliced smoked deli turkey
2 cups	prepared brown gravy
1½ cups	grated cheddar cheese

Preheat broiler.

Arrange the rolls on a baking sheet and toast under the broiler until lightly golden. Remove from oven and top each roll with 2 pieces bacon and one-sixth of the smoked turkey. Drizzle each with ⅓ cup gravy and sprinkle with ¼ cup cheese. Return to the broiler and cook just until cheese melts. Serve immediately.

#58

Grilled Tomato, Bacon, and Cheese Sandwiches

MAKES 4 SERVINGS

¼ cup	butter or margarine, softened
8 slices	sourdough bread
2 tablespoons	mayonnaise
8 slices	American cheese
8 thick slices	fresh tomato
8 strips	bacon, cooked

Heat a large frying pan over medium heat. Spread butter onto one side of each slice of bread. Lay 4 slices of bread, butter-side down, in the frying pan. Spread top of bread with mayonnaise and top with 1 slice cheese, 2 slices tomato, 2 strips bacon, and another slice cheese. Cover with a slice of bread, butter-side out. Fry sandwiches until golden on both sides.

Cheesy Bacon Caesar Wraps

MAKES 4 SERVINGS

½ cup	whipped cream cheese
4 (10-inch)	flour tortillas
2 cups	shredded romaine lettuce
¼ cup	Caesar salad dressing
8	large fresh basil leaves
8 strips	bacon, cooked
2	Roma tomatoes, thinly sliced
¼ cup	grated Parmesan cheese

Spread the cream cheese evenly over one side of each tortilla. In a bowl, toss the lettuce with the salad dressing, then spread the salad down the center of the tortillas. Top each with 2 basil leaves, 2 pieces crumbled bacon, and several tomato slices; sprinkle with the cheese. Roll up tightly, jelly-roll style, and cut in half on the diagonal.

Chicken, Bacon, and Guacamole Sandwiches

MAKES 4 SERVINGS

8 slices	**foccacia bread**
³⁄4 cup	**guacamole**
¹⁄2 pound	**sliced roasted chicken**
8 strips	**bacon, cooked and cut in half**
4 slices	**pepper Jack cheese**
4 slices	**tomato**
4 pieces	**lettuce**
¹⁄4 cup	**ranch dressing**

Spread the bread slices with the guacamole. On 4 pieces of bread, layer the chicken, bacon, cheese, tomato, and lettuce. Drizzle lettuce with the dressing and top with remaining bread slices, guacamole-side down. Press together and cut in half diagonally.

Turkey, Bacon, Pesto, and Havarti Paninis

MAKES 4 SERVINGS

4	**ciabatta rolls, split (or 8 slices Italian bread)**
½ cup	**pesto**
8 thin slices	**Havarti cheese**
8 strips	**cooked bacon, cut in half**
½ pound	**shaved deli turkey breast**
1 tablespoon	**olive oil**

Spread the insides of the rolls with pesto. Top 4 halves with 1 cheese slice, 2 strips bacon, one-fourth of the turkey, and another slice of cheese. Replace with top halves of rolls and brush the outsides of rolls with the oil.

Heat a frying pan or double-sided sandwich maker on medium-high. Arrange sandwiches in pan, in batches if necessary, and use a heavy frying pan, bacon press, or foil-wrapped brick to flatten the sandwiches. Grill until golden brown, about 2–3 minutes on each side, or until cheese is melted and bread is golden. (If using a sandwich maker, grill for 3–4 minutes.) Cut each sandwich in half diagonally and serve.

Egg Salad Croissants

MAKES 6 SERVINGS

12	hard-boiled eggs, peeled and finely chopped
2/3 cup	mayonnaise
1 1/2 teaspoons	mustard
1 teaspoon	minced fresh parsley
1/4 teaspoon	salt
1/4 teaspoon	pepper
6 strips	bacon, cooked and crumbled
6	iceberg or romaine lettuce leaves
6	large croissants, split

In a bowl, combine the eggs, mayonnaise, mustard, parsley, salt, and pepper; mix well. Cover and refrigerate for at least 1 hour. Just before serving, stir in the crumbled bacon. Spread about 1/2 cup egg salad on the bottom half of each croissant and top with a lettuce leaf and top half of croissant.

Bacon, Turkey, and Red Pepper Subs

MAKES 4 SERVINGS

4	**French rolls, split**
2 tablespoons	**butter or margarine, softened**
¼ cup	**mayonnaise**
1 jar (7 ounces)	**roasted red peppers, drained**
½ pound	**shaved smoked deli turkey**
8 strips	**bacon, cooked and crumbled**
2 cups	**shredded lettuce**
	salt and pepper, to taste

Preheat broiler.

Arrange French rolls cut-side up on a baking sheet and toast under the broiler until lightly golden. Remove from oven and spread half of each roll with butter; spread remaining halves with mayonnaise. Layer the red peppers, turkey, bacon, and lettuce on 4 halves and sprinkle with salt and pepper. Top with remaining roll halves and serve.

Cuban Sandwiches

MAKES 4 SERVINGS

4	soft hoagie rolls, split
2 tablespoons	butter or margarine, softened
1 tablespoon	mustard
4	large dill pickles, horizontally sliced
1 pound	thinly sliced roasted pork
½ pound	bacon, cooked
½ pound	thinly sliced ham
½ pound	Jarlsburg Swiss cheese, sliced

Spray a cast-iron frying pan, griddle, or double-sided sandwich maker with nonstick cooking spray and heat to medium. Spread one side of each roll with butter and the other with mustard. Layer each sandwich with pickles, pork, bacon, ham, and cheese. Arrange sandwiches in pan, in batches if necessary, and use a heavy frying pan, bacon press, or foil-wrapped brick to flatten. Grill the sandwiches until golden brown, about 2–3 minutes on each side, or until cheese is melted and bread is golden. (If using a double-sided sandwich maker, grill for 3–4 minutes.) Cut in half diagonally and serve.

Bacon Reubens
MAKES 4 SERVINGS

8 slices	marble rye bread
4 tablespoons	Thousand Island salad dressing
8 slices	Swiss cheese
$\frac{1}{2}$ pound	thinly sliced pastrami
1 cup	crisp refrigerated sauerkraut, drained
8 strips	bacon, cooked and cut in half
$\frac{1}{4}$ cup	butter or margarine, softened
$1\frac{1}{2}$ teaspoons	vegetable oil

Spread each slice of bread with Thousand Island dressing. Layer each sandwich with 1 cheese slice, pastrami, sauerkraut, 2 strips bacon, and another slice of cheese. Top with remaining bread slices and spread butter on the outsides of each sandwich. Brush a large frying pan with the oil and heat to medium-high. Grill the sandwiches until golden brown, about 2–3 minutes on each side, or until cheese is melted and bread is crispy.

Shrimp and Bacon Po' Boys

MAKES 4 SERVINGS

2 tablespoons	mayonnaise
1 tablespoon	ranch salad dressing
1½ teaspoons	mustard
1 teaspoon	hot red pepper sauce
¼ teaspoon	pepper
1 cup	grated sharp cheddar cheese
1½ cups	shredded iceberg lettuce
3 strips	bacon, cooked and finely crumbled
4	hoagie buns, split and toasted
16	large shrimp, peeled, deveined, and cooked
2	tomatoes, each cut in 4 slices

In a bowl, combine the mayonnaise, ranch dressing, mustard, red pepper sauce, and pepper. Toss with the cheese, lettuce, and bacon. Divide the mixture among the bottom halves of the rolls and then top each with 4 shrimp, 2 tomato slices, and top halves of rolls. Cut on the diagonal and serve.

#67-76

SIDE
DISHES

Southern-Fried Sweet Corn

MAKES 6 SERVINGS

6 ears	**fresh sweet corn, husked and cleaned**
2 tablespoons	**butter or margarine**
½	**large red bell pepper, seeded and diced**
6 strips	**bacon, cooked and crumbled**
	salt and pepper, to taste

In a bowl, slice the corn off the cob and scrape each cob into the bowl to release the milk. Melt the butter over medium-high heat in a large, deep frying pan. Add the bell pepper and cook until softened. Add the corn and cook, stirring occasionally, until tender. Stir in the bacon, salt, and pepper and cook 1 minute more.

Sautéed Mushrooms

MAKES 6 SERVINGS

½ pound	bacon, chopped
1	medium onion, sliced
1 pound	medium-sized button mushrooms, thinly sliced
	salt and pepper, to taste
2 tablespoons	chopped fresh chives

In a large frying pan, fry the bacon until almost crisp. Add the onion and sauté until tender and lightly browned. Add the mushrooms and sauté until the mushrooms are lightly browned. Sprinkle with salt, pepper, and chives and serve immediately.

Ultimate Bacon and Garlic Mashed Potatoes

MAKES 8 SERVINGS

4 ½ pounds	russet potatoes, peeled
1 package (8 ounces)	cream cheese, room temperature
1 cup	sour cream
1 clove	garlic, minced
1 teaspoon	salt
½ teaspoon	pepper
2	green onions, finely chopped
8 strips	bacon, cooked and crumbled
¼ cup	butter, cut into pieces
¼ teaspoon	paprika

Preheat oven to 400 degrees and butter a baking dish.

Boil potatoes in a large pot of water until fork tender. Drain potatoes and mash well; set aside.

In a bowl, beat the cream cheese and sour cream until smooth with an electric mixer. Gradually add potatoes, garlic, salt, and pepper, beating until smooth. Stir in the onions and bacon. Spread mixture into the prepared baking dish. Dot with butter and sprinkle with paprika. Cover and bake until heated through, about 35–45 minutes.

#70

Twice-Baked Sweet Potatoes with Candied Bacon

MAKES 8 SERVINGS

¹/₂ cup	packed brown sugar, divided
8 strips	bacon
4	large sweet potatoes
4 tablespoons	butter or margarine, melted
1 teaspoon	ground cinnamon
1 teaspoon	salt
¹/₂ teaspoon	pepper

Preheat oven to 400 degrees.

Line a baking sheet with foil and place a wire rack on top; spray the rack with nonstick cooking spray. Spread ¹/₄ cup brown sugar on a plate and coat both sides of each bacon slice. Lay bacon strips on rack and bake until crispy, about 15 minutes; remove from rack, cool, and finely chop.

Grease a baking sheet and set aside. Scrub potatoes and pierce each with a fork two or three times. Bake for 1 hour or until fork tender. When cool enough to handle, split potatoes lengthwise and carefully scoop out cooked potato into a bowl, leaving a ¹/₄-inch shell. Mash the potato with the butter, cinnamon, salt, pepper, and remaining ¹/₂ cup brown sugar until smooth. Return potato mixture to shells and sprinkle candied bacon over top. Transfer to the greased baking sheet and bake for 20 minutes.

Creamy Broccoli-Bacon Bake

MAKES 6 SERVINGS

2 pounds	fresh broccoli florets
1/4 cup	butter
1/4 cup	flour
3/4 cup	chicken broth or stock
1 cup	half-and-half
2 tablespoons	sherry (optional)
2 tablespoons	lemon juice
1/4 teaspoon	salt
1/4 teaspoon	pepper
12 strips	bacon, cooked and crumbled
1/2 cup	grated cheddar cheese

Steam broccoli over boiling water until crisp-tender, about
5 minutes. Drain and transfer to a greased 9 x 13-inch baking
dish. Melt butter in a heavy saucepan over low heat. Blend in
flour, stirring until smooth, and cook 1 minute, stirring constantly.
Increase heat to medium and gradually add chicken broth and
half-and-half, stirring constantly, until thickened and bubbly.
Stir in sherry, if using, lemon juice, salt, and pepper. Pour sauce
over broccoli and sprinkle with bacon and cheese. Bake for
25–30 minutes or until top is lightly browned.

Baked Beans

MAKES 8 SERVINGS

1 pound	**bacon, cut into 1-inch pieces**
1	**medium onion, chopped**
1 clove	**garlic, minced**
2 cans (15 ounces each)	**pork and beans in tomato sauce**
½ cup	**packed brown sugar**
½ cup	**ketchup**
2 teaspoons	**mustard**

Preheat oven to 350 degrees and grease a 2-quart casserole dish.

In a large frying pan over medium heat, cook bacon until crispy and remove with a slotted spoon. Drain on paper towels; discard all but 1 tablespoon bacon drippings in pan. Cook the onion in the drippings over medium heat for 5 minutes, or until soft. Add garlic and cook 1 minute more. Add the pork and beans and bacon and stir.

In a bowl, combine the brown sugar, ketchup, and mustard. Add the mixture to the beans and stir; transfer to the prepared baking dish. Bake, uncovered, for 50–60 minutes or until beans are bubbling.

#73

Skillet Bacon Cornbread

MAKES 8 SERVINGS

1½ cups	cornmeal
½ cup	flour
2 teaspoons	baking powder
1 teaspoon	sugar
1 teaspoon	salt
¼ teaspoon	baking soda
¼ cup	vegetable oil
1½ cups	buttermilk
2	eggs, beaten
6 strips	bacon

Preheat oven to 425 degrees.

In a bowl, whisk together the cornmeal, flour, baking powder, sugar, salt, and baking soda. Make a well in the dry ingredients and add oil, buttermilk, and eggs; stir until just combined.

In a medium-sized cast-iron skillet or frying pan with an oven-safe handle, cook the bacon over medium heat until crispy. Transfer the bacon to paper towels and crumble. Pour out all but 1 tablespoon of the bacon drippings from the skillet and heat over medium. Add the crumbled bacon to the batter and stir until just combined; pour quickly into the hot skillet and bake for 20–25 minutes or until golden brown and center springs back when lightly pressed. Cool and cut into wedges.

Squash Casserole

MAKES 8 SERVINGS

3 tablespoons	butter, divided
4 cups	sliced yellow squash
1/2 cup	chopped onion
35	buttery round crackers, crushed
1 cup	grated cheddar cheese
6 strips	bacon, cooked and finely crumbled
2	eggs, beaten
3/4 cup	milk
1/4 cup	butter or margarine, melted
1/2 teaspoon	salt
1/4 teaspoon	pepper

Preheat oven to 400 degrees and grease a 9 x 13-inch baking dish.

Melt 1 tablespoon butter in a frying pan over medium heat. Add squash and onion and stir; cover and cook until squash is tender, about 5 minutes. Drain any liquid and transfer to a large bowl; reserve.

In a separate bowl, combine the crackers, cheese, and bacon. Stir half of the cracker mixture into the squash mixture. In another bowl, combine eggs and milk and add to squash mixture. Stir in 1/4 cup melted butter, and season with salt and pepper. Spread into the prepared baking dish. Sprinkle with remaining cracker mixture and dot with the remaining 2 tablespoons butter , cut in pieces. Bake for 25 minutes, or until lightly browned.

Better Bacon and Green Bean Casserole

MAKES 6 SERVINGS

3 cups	fresh green beans, ends trimmed
2 tablespoons	butter
1	small onion, chopped
6 strips	bacon, cooked and crumbled
1/3 cup	mayonnaise
1/3 cup	sour cream
1/2 cup	grated cheddar cheese
1/4 teaspoon	salt
1/2 teaspoon	pepper

Preheat oven to 325 degrees and grease a 1 1/2-quart baking dish.

Bring a pot of water to a boil, add green beans, and cook for 7–8 minutes, or until tender; drain and reserve.

In a frying pan over medium heat, melt the butter and sauté the onion until lightly browned. Add the green beans and bacon and stir.

In a bowl, combine the mayonnaise, sour cream, cheese, salt, and pepper. Stir the mixture into the beans and transfer to the prepared baking dish. Bake for 20 minutes, or until heated through and lightly browned.

Deviled Eggs with Bacon

MAKES 16 EGGS

8	hard-boiled eggs, peeled
1/3 cup	mayonnaise
1 teaspoon	mustard
1/2 teaspoon	curry powder
	salt and pepper, to taste
6 strips	bacon, cooked and finely crumbled

Cut each egg in half lengthwise; gently scoop out yolks and place in a bowl. Mash yolks with a fork, then stir in mayonnaise, mustard, and curry powder until well blended. Add salt and pepper. Spoon or pipe about 1 tablespoon yolk mixture into the hollow of each egg half. Serve immediately or cover and chill up to 4 hours, garnishing with crumbled bacon just before serving.

DINNERS

Barbecue Chicken and Bacon Pizza

MAKES 4 SERVINGS

⅓ to ½ cup	barbecue sauce
1 (12-inch-round)	prebaked Italian pizza crust
¾ cup	chopped cooked chicken breast
8 strips	bacon, cooked and crumbled
1¼ cups	grated cheddar cheese
¼ cup	finely sliced red onion (optional)

Preheat oven to 425 degrees.

Spread the barbecue sauce on the crust and sprinkle with the chicken, bacon, cheese, and onion, if using. Bake for 8–10 minutes, or until cheese is bubbly. Remove from the oven, cut into 8 wedges, and serve.

Asparagus, Bacon, and Caramelized Onion Pizza

MAKES 4 SERVINGS

8 strips	bacon, cut into 1-inch pieces
1	medium onion, chopped
1 cup	chopped fresh asparagus
8 ounces	prepared pizza dough
4	Roma tomatoes, thinly sliced
1 pound	grated mozzarella cheese
	pepper, to taste
1/3 cup	grated Parmesan cheese

Preheat oven to 375 degrees.

Cook bacon in a frying pan over medium-high heat until partially cooked but still flexible; remove to paper towels to drain. Drain all but 1 tablespoon bacon drippings. Over low heat, cook the onion in the drippings until golden brown and caramelized, about 20 minutes. Add the asparagus and cook for 3 minutes more; remove from heat and reserve.

Press or roll pizza dough into a 12-inch circle and fit in a pizza pan. Top with the tomatoes, asparagus-onion mixture, mozzarella cheese, and bacon. Sprinkle with pepper and Parmesan cheese. Bake for 15–20 minutes, or until the crust is golden brown. Cool for 5 minutes before slicing and serving.

Bacon Cheeseburger Meatloaf

MAKES 6–8 SERVINGS

8 strips	bacon
1	small onion, finely chopped
1½ pounds	lean ground beef
1	egg, lightly beaten
¼ cup	evaporated milk
½ teaspoon	salt
¼ teaspoon	pepper
8 ounces	Colby cheese, grated and divided
½ cup	seasoned breadcrumbs

Preheat oven to 350 degrees.

In a frying pan, cook bacon over medium heat until browned; remove with a slotted spoon, drain on paper towels, and crumble. Discard all but 1 tablespoon of the bacon drippings. Stir in the onion and cook until soft; remove from heat.

In a bowl, stir together the beef, egg, milk, salt, and pepper. Stir in the onion, two-thirds of the cheese, and all but 1 tablespoon bacon. Stir in breadcrumbs and mix until well blended. Shape into a loaf and transfer to a shallow baking dish. Bake for 1 hour. Drain fat and sprinkle with remaining cheese and bacon. Return to oven and bake until cheese is melted, about 5 minutes more.

Macaroni and Cheese

MAKES 4 SERVINGS

1 package (8 ounces)	uncooked elbow macaroni
4 tablespoons	butter or margarine
4 tablespoons	flour
1 cup	milk
1 cup	half-and-half
2 tablespoons	grated onion
2 cups	grated sharp cheddar cheese
8 strips	bacon, cooked and crumbled, divided
	salt and pepper, to taste

Preheat oven to 400 degrees and butter a 2-quart baking dish.

Cook macaroni in boiling salted water according to package directions. While macaroni is cooking, melt the butter in a saucepan over medium heat. Slowly whisk in the flour, stirring until blended. Slowly add the milk, half-and-half, and onion, stirring constantly. Heat until mixture bubbles and cook for 2 minutes more. Reduce heat and continue cooking for 10 minutes, stirring constantly. Add cheese, a little at a time, and continue to cook over low heat until cheese is melted. Add all but 1 tablespoon bacon, stir, and add salt and pepper. Add cooked, drained macaroni and mix well.

Spread into the prepared baking dish, top with reserved bacon, and bake for 20 minutes or until top is lightly browned and bubbling.

Farfalle with Broccoli and Bacon

MAKES 4 SERVINGS

1 package (8 ounces)	uncooked farfalle pasta
8 strips	bacon, cut into 1-inch pieces
2 cups	broccoli florets
2 cloves	garlic, minced
2 cups	grated mozzarella cheese
1/4 cup	grated Parmesan cheese
	salt and pepper, to taste
1/4 cup	chopped fresh parsley

Cook pasta in boiling water according to package directions. Meanwhile, cook the bacon in a frying pan over medium heat until just starting to brown. Drain off all but 1 tablespoon of the bacon drippings, add the broccoli and garlic, and cook until the broccoli is slightly tender, stirring often, about 4–5 minutes. Reduce heat to low; drain the pasta and add it to the pan. Heat through and add the cheeses, salt, pepper, and parsley. Stir gently, just until the cheese begins to melt, and serve at once.

Bacon-Wrapped Orange Chicken

MAKES 4 SERVINGS

4	**boneless skinless chicken breasts**
¼ teaspoon	**dried sage**
¼ teaspoon	**dried thyme**
	salt and pepper, to taste
4 strips	**bacon, partially cooked**
¼ cup	**butter or margarine, melted**
½ cup	**orange marmalade**

Preheat oven to 350 degrees and line a shallow baking pan with nonstick foil.

Sprinkle each chicken breast evenly with the sage, thyme, salt, and pepper. Wrap each chicken breast with 1 slice bacon and arrange in the prepared baking pan with bacon ends tucked under.

Melt together the butter and marmalade in a saucepan over medium heat and stir until combined. Pour over bacon-wrapped chicken breasts. Bake, uncovered, for 45–50 minutes, or until bacon is crisp and chicken is done.

Easy Bacon Chicken Rolls

MAKES 4 SERVINGS

4	**boneless skinless chicken breasts**
1 package (5 ounces)	**garlic and herb spreadable cheese, such as Boursin, softened**
1 package (2.1 ounces)	**precooked bacon**

Preheat oven to 350 degrees and grease a 2-quart baking dish.

Pound each chicken breast between two sheets of plastic wrap to a thickness of $\frac{1}{4}$ inch. Spread each piece of chicken with the cheese and roll up like a jelly roll. Wrap each piece of chicken in several pieces of bacon and secure with toothpicks. Arrange in the prepared dish and bake for 45 minutes.

Fettuccini Carbonara

MAKES 4–6 SERVINGS

2	**eggs, lightly beaten**
¼ cup	**half-and-half**
¼ teaspoon	**pepper**
½ pound	**bacon, chopped**
2 cloves	**garlic, minced**
1 teaspoon	**salt**
1 pound	**uncooked fettuccini**
3 ounces	**grated Parmesan cheese**
½ cup	**loosely packed flat-leaf parsley leaves, finely chopped**

Put a large pot filled with water over high heat to boil. Meanwhile, whisk the eggs, half-and-half, and pepper in a bowl; reserve.

Cook bacon in a frying pan over medium-high heat, stirring occasionally, until lightly brown. Drain off all but 1 tablespoon bacon drippings; add garlic and cook, stirring, until fragrant, about 1 minute. Remove from heat and set aside.

Cook fettuccini in the boiling water until tender to the bite. Drain well and immediately pour pasta back into the pot and add the egg mixture. Toss to thoroughly coat pasta with eggs. Add the bacon-garlic mixture, cheese, and parsley and toss to combine thoroughly. Adjust seasonings, if needed. Serve hot.

Chicken and Bacon Pockets

MAKES 4 SERVINGS

4 ounces	cream cheese, room temperature
2 tablespoons	milk
2 cups	cooked, chopped chicken
8 strips	bacon, cooked and crumbled
¼ teaspoon	pepper
2 cans (8 ounces each)	refrigerated crescent rolls
2 tablespoons	butter or margarine, melted
1 tablespoon	sesame seeds

Preheat oven to 350 degrees.

In a bowl, mix the cream cheese and milk until smooth; add the chicken, bacon, and pepper and stir until combined. Unroll crescent rolls and separate dough into 8 rectangles, pressing along the diagonal perforations to seal. Equally divide the filling and spoon on the bottom half of each dough rectangle. Fold dough over the filling, pinch the edges to seal, and crimp edges with a fork. Brush each pocket with melted butter and sprinkle with sesame seeds. Transfer to a baking sheet and bake for 15 minutes, or until golden brown.

Salmon with Bacon, Shallots, and Dill

MAKES 4 SERVINGS

1 tablespoon	butter or margarine
1	large shallot, finely chopped
8 strips	bacon, diced
1 tablespoon	chopped fresh dill
2 tablespoons	lemon juice
4	wild salmon fillets (about 6 ounces each)

Preheat oven to 400 degrees.

Cut a piece of aluminum foil double the size of a 9 x 13-inch baking dish and fit one half of it in the dish; spray with nonstick cooking spray.

Over medium heat, melt the butter in a large sauté pan and cook the shallot until softened. Add the bacon and cook until light golden brown. Add the dill and lemon juice and cook for 1 minute; remove from heat. Arrange the salmon fillets on the foil in the baking dish and spoon the bacon mixture over top. Fold the other half of the foil over the fish and crimp the edges to make a packet. Bake for about 20 minutes, or until salmon is opaque and flakes easily when tested with a fork.

Maple-Bacon Drumsticks
MAKES 4 SERVINGS

8	chicken drumsticks
½ teaspoon	pepper
8 strips	bacon
¼ cup	maple syrup
1½ teaspoons	Worcestershire sauce
¼ cup	ketchup
2 cloves	garlic, minced

Preheat oven to 375 degrees and generously grease a 9 x 13-inch baking dish.

Sprinkle the drumsticks with pepper. Wrap a strip of bacon tightly around each drumstick, securing ends with toothpicks. Combine the maple syrup, Worcestershire sauce, ketchup, and garlic in a bowl and brush the mixture over the drumsticks, coating all sides. Arrange in the prepared baking dish and bake for 50–60 minutes, turning drumsticks once, until the thickest part of the chicken registers 160 degrees on a meat thermometer.

#88

Crispy Bacon Fried Rice

MAKES 6 SERVINGS

8 strips	**bacon, diced**
½ pound	**lean pork, cut into ½-inch cubes**
½ cup	**chopped celery**
½ cup	**chopped onion**
2	**green onions, chopped**
3 cups	**cold cooked rice**
1 tablespoon	**soy sauce**
2	**eggs, lightly beaten**

In a frying pan over medium heat, cook the bacon, pork, celery, and onion until the bacon is browned and vegetables are tender. Add the rice and soy sauce and cook for 3 minutes, stirring constantly. Pour the eggs over the rice in a stream, stirring constantly, and cook just until eggs are cooked. Remove from heat and serve at once.

Bacon Steak Rolls

MAKES 4 SERVINGS

1½ pounds	top beef round steak, ¼ inch thick and cut in 4 equal pieces
½ teaspoon	salt
¼ teaspoon	pepper
6 strips	bacon
¼ cup	finely chopped onion
4 tablespoons	flour, divided
1 cup	beef stock or broth

Preheat oven to 350 degrees.

Place slices of meat, one at a time, on a board and pound with a flat mallet without breaking the flesh; season with salt and pepper and reserve.

In a large, heavy Dutch oven, fry bacon until crisp; reserve drippings and remove bacon to drain on paper towels, then crumble. Sprinkle the bacon and onion evenly over the 4 steaks. Starting at the narrow end, roll each steak up like a jelly roll and secure with a piece of string. Coat rolls with 2 tablespoons flour. Heat the bacon drippings over medium heat and brown the meat rolls. Remove from heat, cover, and bake for 1½ hours or until tender. Remove steak rolls from pan with a slotted spoon and reserve; drain excess fat from Dutch oven but do not wipe clean.

In a bowl, whisk remaining 2 tablespoons flour in beef stock until combined and add mixture slowly to Dutch oven. Simmer mixture over medium-high heat, stirring constantly, until sauce thickens and comes to a boil. Add steak rolls to sauce; simmer 5 minutes. Remove from heat and serve rolls accompanied with sauce.

Bacon-Wrapped Steaks with Bacon-Chive Butter

MAKES 8 SERVINGS

3/4 cup	butter, softened
2 tablespoons	chopped fresh chives
2 pieces	bacon, cooked and finely crumbled
1 clove	garlic, minced
1/4 cup	soy sauce
2 tablespoons	olive oil
2 tablespoons	ketchup
1/4 teaspoon	dry mustard
1 clove	garlic, minced
4	beef rib-eye steaks, cut 1 inch thick (8 to 10 ounces each) pepper, to taste
8 strips	bacon, partially cooked

To make herb butter, in a bowl, combine the butter, chives, bacon, and garlic. Scoop on a piece of plastic wrap and roll into a cylinder. Twist ends of plastic wrap. Refrigerate for at least 4 hours.

In a shallow dish or ziplock plastic bag, combine the soy sauce, oil, ketchup, dry mustard, and garlic. Add meat and marinate for 4 hours, turning several times.

Preheat grill and season steaks with the pepper. Wrap the edge of each steak with 2 strips of bacon, securing ends with toothpicks. Grill steaks to desired doneness, turning once halfway through grilling. Slice butter cylinder into 8 pieces and top each hot steak with a pat of herb butter.

Cheesy Bacon Dogs

MAKES 6 SERVINGS

6	premium all-beef franks
6 slices	cheddar cheese, cut in thirds
6 thick-cut strips	bacon
6	hot dog buns

Grease and preheat grill for indirect medium heat.

Cut a slit about three-fourths of the way through each hot dog and stuff each pocket with cheese. Wrap a strip of bacon tightly around each hot dog, securing with toothpicks at each end. Arrange the hot dogs over indirect heat and grill, turning every few minutes, until bacon is completely cooked, about 20 minutes. During the last minute of cooking, open up the hot dog buns and place them open-side down on the grill to lightly toast. Remove the hot dogs and buns from the grill. Remove the toothpicks from the hot dogs, place hot dogs in the buns, and serve.

Creamy Seafood and Bacon Pasta

MAKES 6 SERVINGS

4 strips	bacon, diced
2	large shallots, minced
½ pound	baby shrimp
½ pound	scallops
⅔ cup	heavy cream
1 tablespoon	tomato paste
¼ cup	grated Parmesan cheese
¼ cup	chopped flat-leaf parsley, leaves only
¼ teaspoon	pepper
1 pound	fresh linguine

Bring a large pot of salted water to a boil. Meanwhile, cook the bacon in a sauté pan over medium heat until lightly browned. Add the shallots and cook for several minutes until translucent. Add the shrimp and scallops and cook until shrimp are pink and scallops are opaque, about 3–5 minutes. Add the cream and tomato paste, and cook until slightly thickened. Add half of the cheese, parsley, and pepper and stir. Cook the pasta in the boiling water until tender; drain. Toss pasta with the sauce and serve topped with the remaining Parmesan cheese.

Bacon-Wrapped Pork Chops

MAKES 6 SERVINGS

12 strips	**bacon**
6 (1-inch-thick)	**boneless pork chops**
½ cup	**grated Colby cheese**

Preheat oven to 350 degrees and grease a 9 x 13-inch baking dish.

Fry the bacon in a frying pan over medium heat until cooked through but still flexible. Remove the bacon and quickly sear the pork chops in the pan drippings until browned. Drain on paper towels and wrap 2 strips of bacon around each pork chop. Arrange in the prepared baking dish and bake for 45 minutes. Sprinkle with cheese and bake for 15 more minutes.

Baked Spaghetti with Bacon

MAKES 4–6 SERVINGS

½ pound	**bacon, diced**
1	**medium onion, diced**
1 clove	**garlic, minced**
1 can (14.5 ounces)	**diced tomatoes with liquid**
1 can (8 ounces)	**tomato sauce**
½ teaspoon	**dried oregano, crumbled**
1 package (8 ounces)	**spaghetti, cooked and drained**
¼ cup	**grated Parmesan cheese**

Preheat oven to 350 degrees.

In a frying pan over medium heat, brown bacon and onion until bacon is crisp. Drain all but about 1 teaspoon bacon drippings from the pan and add the garlic; sauté for 1 minute. Add the tomatoes, tomato sauce, and oregano; bring to a boil. Spread cooked spaghetti in a 9 x 13-inch baking dish. Pour sauce over top and sprinkle with cheese. Cover with foil and bake for 45 minutes.

No-Stir Risotto with Peas and Bacon

MAKES 4 SERVINGS

2 tablespoons	olive oil
1 tablespoon	butter or margarine
1	onion, finely chopped
2 cups	Arborio or short-grain rice
4 cups	chicken stock or broth
1 cup	frozen peas
6 strips	bacon, cooked and finely crumbled
½ teaspoon	salt
¼ teaspoon	pepper
½ cup	grated Parmesan cheese

Heat the oil and butter in a sauté pan over medium heat; add the onion and fry until lightly browned, about 5–7 minutes. Add the rice and cook for 2 minutes, stirring to coat grains with oil. Add the chicken stock and bring to a boil. Stir well, reduce heat, and cook, covered, for 15–20 minutes, or until the rice is almost tender. Stir in the peas, bacon, salt, and pepper; cook for 3 minutes, or until the peas are tender. Sprinkle with Parmesan cheese and serve.

DESSERTS

Bacon–Chocolate Chip Cookies

MAKES 2 ½ DOZEN

2 ¼ cups	flour
1 teaspoon	baking soda
¼ teaspoon	salt
1 cup	butter or margarine, softened
¾ cup	sugar
¾ cup	packed brown sugar
1 teaspoon	vanilla
2	eggs
10 strips	bacon, cooked and finely chopped
2 cups	semisweet chocolate chips

Preheat oven to 375 degrees and lightly grease a baking sheet.

In a bowl, whisk together the flour, baking soda, and salt; reserve. Beat butter, sugars, and vanilla in a large bowl until creamy. Add eggs, one at a time, beating well after each addition. Gradually add the flour mixture, beating until combined. Stir in bacon and chocolate chips and drop by rounded tablespoonfuls on the prepared baking sheet, about 2 inches apart. Bake for 10–12 minutes or until golden brown. Remove to cooling rack and cool completely. Store in refrigerator and bring to room temperature before serving.

Bacon–Corn Flake Cookies

MAKES ABOUT 3 DOZEN COOKIES

½ cup	butter or margarine
¾ cup	packed brown sugar
1	egg
1 cup	flour
¼ teaspoon	baking soda
½ pound	bacon, cooked and crumbled
2 cups	corn flakes
½ cup	golden raisins

Preheat oven to 350 degrees and grease a baking sheet.

Melt butter over low heat in a small saucepan. Add sugar and stir until it dissolves; remove from heat and cool briefly. Beat in egg.

In a bowl, whisk together the flour and baking soda; add to egg mixture and stir until combined. Stir in bacon, corn flakes, and raisins. Drop by rounded teaspoonfuls on the prepared baking sheet, about 2 inches apart. Bake for 14–18 minutes, or until edges are lightly browned. Remove to cooling rack and cool completely. Store in refrigerator and bring to room temperature before serving.

Peanut Butter–Bacon Cupcakes
MAKES 24 CUPCAKES

1 pound	sliced bacon
2 1/2 cups	creamy peanut butter, divided
1/4 cup	butter or margarine, softened
4	eggs
1 box	yellow cake mix
2/3 cup	water
2 packages (8 ounces each)	cream cheese, room temperature
5 cups	powdered sugar
1/4 cup	heavy cream

Preheat oven to 350 degrees and line 2 cupcake pans with paper liners.

Cook the bacon in a frying pan over medium heat until browned; reserve 1/4 cup bacon drippings. Drain bacon on paper towels and crumble. Beat 1/2 cup peanut butter, reserved bacon drippings, and butter with an electric mixer in a bowl until light and fluffy. Add the eggs, one at a time, beating after each addition. Add the cake mix and water, and mix until just blended. Fold in two-thirds of the bacon. Pour the batter into prepared cupcake pans, about two-thirds full. Bake 20–25 minutes, or until a toothpick inserted into the center of a cupcake comes out clean; cool on a wire rack.

In a bowl, beat the remaining 2 cups peanut butter and cream cheese together with an electric mixer until creamy. Gradually add the powdered sugar, alternating with the cream, until frosting is of spreading consistency (you may not need all of the cream). Spread the frosting over the cooled cupcakes and garnish with the reserved crumbled bacon.

Chocolate-Covered Bacon Toffee

MAKES ABOUT 1 1/2 POUNDS

1 cup	sugar
1 cup	butter or margarine
1/4 cup	water
1/4 teaspoon	salt
1 teaspoon	vanilla
6 strips	bacon, cooked and finely chopped
1 cup	semisweet chocolate chips

Line a baking sheet with a silicone liner or parchment paper.

In a heavy-bottomed saucepan, combine the sugar, butter, water, and salt. Attach a candy thermometer to the side of the pan, making sure the bulb doesn't rest on the bottom of the pan. Stir frequently and boil the mixture about 20 minutes or until it reaches 290 degrees.

Remove from the heat and quickly stir in the vanilla and bacon. Immediately pour the mixture onto the prepared baking sheet and spread with a spatula to about 1/4 inch to 1/2 inch thickness. While the toffee is still hot, sprinkle the surface with the chocolate chips. When the chips start to turn shiny, spread the chocolate to the edges with the spatula. Cool until hard and then break the toffee into chunks. Store in an airtight container in the refrigerator.

Butterscotch Pudding with Candied Bacon

MAKES 4 SERVINGS

½ pound	sliced bacon
2 tablespoons	brown sugar
¾ cup	dark brown sugar
3 tablespoons	cornstarch
¼ teaspoon	salt
1 cup	evaporated milk
2 cups	whole milk
3	egg yolks
3 tablespoons	butter or margarine
1½ teaspoons	vanilla
	whipped cream

Preheat oven to 425 degrees and line a large rimmed baking sheet with foil.

Arrange the bacon in a single layer in the pan. Bake for 10 minutes and drain grease. Sprinkle the brown sugar over the bacon. Bake for 5–10 minutes more or until bacon is crisp; drain on paper towels. Finely chop candied bacon and reserve.

In a saucepan, whisk together dark brown sugar, cornstarch, and salt. Add both milks and cook over medium heat, stirring constantly, until thickened and bubbly. Continue cooking and stirring 2 minutes more; remove from heat. Stir a small amount of the hot mixture into egg yolks and quickly whisk; pour back into hot mixture and cook, stirring constantly, 2 minutes more. Remove from heat and stir in butter and vanilla. Cool for 10 minutes, then pour into bowls. Refrigerate for at least 2 hours and sprinkle with candied bacon. Serve topped with whipped cream.

Chocolate-Glazed Bacon Brownies

MAKES 16 BROWNIES

¹⁄₂ **pound**	**bacon, diced**
¹⁄₄ **to** ¹⁄₃ **cup**	**butter or margarine, melted**
2 (1-ounce) squares	**unsweetened chocolate**
1¹⁄₄ **cups**	**sugar**
2	**eggs**
2 teaspoons	**vanilla**
pinch	**salt**
¹⁄₂ **cup**	**flour**
¹⁄₂ **cup**	**heavy cream**
1 cup	**semisweet chocolate chips**

Preheat oven to 325 degrees and grease an 8 x 8-inch baking pan.

Cook bacon in a frying pan over medium heat and drain, reserving bacon drippings. Pour bacon drippings into a measuring cup and add melted butter to make ¹⁄₂ cup; reserve.

Melt unsweetened chocolate in a saucepan over medium heat and add butter mixture. Remove from heat and stir in sugar until combined. Add the eggs, vanilla, and salt and beat well. Fold in flour and mix just until smooth. Spread half the brownie batter into the prepared baking pan. Sprinkle with half the bacon, and spoon the rest of the batter evenly over top. Bake for 30–35 minutes, or until a toothpick comes out clean.

Heat cream in a small pan over medium heat until simmering. Immediately remove from heat and add chocolate chips, whisking until melted and smooth. Drizzle the mixture on the brownies and sprinkle with the remaining bacon. Cool and cut into squares; store in refrigerator.

NOTES

NOTES

NOTES

NOTES

NOTES

Metric Conversion Chart

VOLUME MEASUREMENTS		WEIGHT MEASUREMENTS		TEMPERATURE CONVERSION	
U.S.	Metric	U.S.	Metric	Fahrenheit	Celsius
1 teaspoon	5 ml	½ ounce	15 g	250	120
1 tablespoon	15 ml	1 ounce	30 g	300	150
¼ cup	60 ml	3 ounces	90 g	325	160
⅓ cup	75 ml	4 ounces	115 g	350	180
½ cup	125 ml	8 ounces	225 g	375	190
⅔ cup	150 ml	12 ounces	350 g	400	200
¾ cup	175 ml	1 pound	450 g	425	220
1 cup	250 ml	2¼ pounds	1 kg	450	230

MORE 101 THINGS® IN THESE

FAVORITES

CAKE MIX
CASSEROLE
RAMEN NOODLES
SLOW COOKER
SMOKER

Each 128 pages, $12.99

Available at bookstores or directly from Gibbs Smith
1.800.835.4993
www.gibbs-smith.com

Gibbs Smith

About the Author

Eliza Cross is an award-winning author and journalist. She also develops recipes and styles cuisine for corporate and print media. Eliza is the founder of the BENSA Bacon Lovers Society. She lives in Centennial, Colorado.